GREEK AND ROMAN TOPICS: 3

*Slavery*

# GREEK AND ROMAN TOPICS
Series Editor: Robin Barrow

*Temples, Priests and Worship*
John Sharwood Smith

*Sparta*
Robin Barrow

*Slavery*
Kenneth Hughes

*Work in Ancient Greece and Rome*
David Taylor

*Athletics, Sports and Games*
John Murrell

## Forthcoming:

*Acting and the Stage*
David Taylor

*Food and Drink*
Kenneth McLeish

GREEK AND ROMAN TOPICS

# *SLAVERY*

## KENNETH HUGHES

*Head of Classics, Tiffin Boys' School, Kingston*

London
GEORGE ALLEN & UNWIN
Boston          Sydney

First published in 1975
Second impression 1977

ISBN 0 04 930004 0

Printed in Great Britain
in 11 point Plantin
by Cox & Wyman Ltd,
London, Fakenham and Reading

# CONTENTS

Acknowledgements *page* 9

Introduction 11

1 *How did you become a slave?* 13

2 *How could you stop being a slave?* 21

3 *What was your status when freed?* 26

4 *What jobs did you do as a slave in Greece?* 30

5 *What jobs did you do as a slave in Rome?* 38

6 *How would you be treated?* 48

7 *Your legal rights, and punishments* 54

8 *How many were there, and who owned them?* 58

Further Study 61

# ILLUSTRATIONS

*Cover :* Scythian knife-sharpener

| | | |
|---|---|---|
| 1 | Slave chain | *page* 13 |
| 2 | Slave on an auction block | 14 |
| 3 | Tombstone of Timotheos | 14 |
| 4 | Hoplites in action | 16 |
| 5 | The Erechtheion | 16 |
| 6 | Tombstone of Regina | 17 |
| 7 | Trimalchio | 18 |
| 8 | *Satyricon* | 22 |
| 9 | Augustus | 24 |
| 10 | Cicero | 27 |
| 11 | The Acropolis | 30 |
| 12 | Socrates | 31 |
| 13 | At the shoemaker's | 31 |
| 14 | Erechtheion building accounts | 32 |
| 15 | School scene | 33 |
| 16a and 16b | Two tombstones | 34 |
| 17 | Picture on a drinking-cup | 34 |
| 18 a | Statuette of a dancing-girl | 36 |
| b | Girl playing a double flute | 36 |
| 19a and 19b | Two gladiator mosaics | 39 |
| 20 | Chariot race from *Ben Hur* | 39 |
| 21 | The Colosseum: exterior view | 40 |
| 22 | Statuette of a negro musician | 41 |
| 23 | Banquet scene from *Satyricon* | 42 |
| 24 | Sleeping slave-boy with lantern | 43 |
| 25 | The Pont du Gard | 44 |
| 26 | Agrippa | 44 |
| 27 | Slave sitting on an altar | 44 |
| 28 | Sale of a piece of cloth | 45 |
| 29 | Sale of cushions | 46 |
| 30 | Pottery works | 46 |
| 31 | The Colosseum: interior view | 56 |
| 32 | The Crucifixion | 57 |

# ACKNOWLEDGEMENTS

I am indebted to the following for permission to reproduce illustrations:
Ashmolean Museum (no. 13); B. T. Batsford Ltd, 15; British Museum (nos 16a, 27); Cambridge University Museum of Archaeology and Ethnology (no. 1); Fellini (nos 7, 8, 23); Galleria Borghese (nos 19a, 19b); Gall. Mus. Vatican (no. 9); Hirmer Fotoarchiv, Munich (no. 4); Mansell Collection (no. 24); Martin v. Wagner Museum (no. 17); Metro-Goldwyn-Mayer (nos 20, 32); Metropolitan Museum of Art, The Cesnola Collection; purchased by subscription 1874-6 (no. 18a); Cliché des Musées Nationaux (no. 26); Museo Provinciale Campano (no. 2); National Archaeological Museum, Athens (nos 14, 16b, 30); Photo Alinari (Cover, nos 10, 12, 28, 29); Photographie Giraudon (no. 22); Jacques Roger (no. 3); M. J. Shortland-Jones (nos 5, 11, 21, 25, 31); South African Cultural History Museum (no. 18b); South Shields Public Libraries and Museums (no. 6).

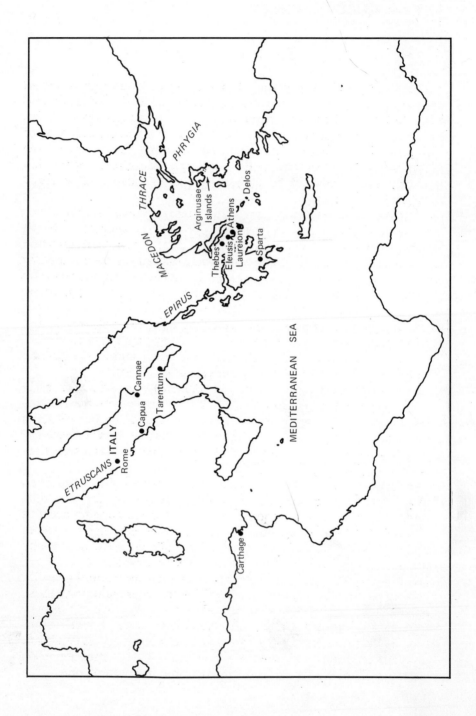

Slavery, that is the ownership of one person by another, is almost unknown nowadays, apart from occasional lurid disclosures about 'white slave trading' and rumours of strange goings on in Arab, African or Oriental countries. It is 140 years since the agitation of Wilberforce and others succeeded in persuading Parliament to free slaves officially throughout the British Empire, despite the opposition of those who thought our textile industry would collapse immediately as a result.

To us slavery is both foreign and repugnant, but throughout the ancient world very few people questioned it or suggested that it might be unnatural. Those people who did think about and question the system either came to the conclusion that slaves were somehow naturally inferior, or else decided that it had been brought about by Fortune, whom both Greeks and Romans came to view as a goddess, and a particularly powerful and fickle one.

In this book I have limited myself to discussing slavery in the periods most commonly studied – the fifth and fourth centuries BC in Greece, with particular reference to Athens, and in the Roman Empire the last two centuries BC and the first two AD.

I have not dealt with slavery in Bronze Age Greece or early Rome, because there is not enough information; or with the Hellenistic Greek world after Alexander the Great and the later Roman Empire, because they could each justify a separate book; or with the *helots* who were peculiar to Sparta, because they are discussed elsewhere in this series, in the volume on Sparta.

Most of the evidence I have used, though not all of it, is confined to the periods I have dealt with. Indeed the sources for this topic present the historian with some difficulty, for we have no account written by a slave telling us what slavery was like, or what slaves thought of their circumstances. Furthermore we have hardly any statistical information, and what there is is unreliable.

As far as Greece is concerned the archaeologists do not have a lot to tell us about slavery, but what they do tell us is quite important. Some tombstones are informative, and so are one or two of the large number of inscriptions left by the Athenians. Greek houses tell us little, except that there was not room in them for many slaves. Books have more to say, though slaves are not often mentioned by historians. They do figure from time to time in lawsuits, one of the favourite occupations of the Athenians, and from the speeches we learn a number of details about the legal position of slaves. There are also essays on various social and economic aspects of Greek life, in which the writers sometimes make comments in passing about some aspect of slavery. For the rest, we are dependent on fiction. Slaves frequently appear in plays, but it is not easy to tell how lifelike their characters are.

For Rome we have rather more information. Once again we have hardly any statistics, and nothing written by slaves about slavery, except that the archaeologist can offer us a large number of tomb-stones. But we do have a fascinating novel, the *Satyricon* by Petronius. Being fiction, it has to be used with care, and even here most of the characters are ex-slaves, rather than slaves. Nevertheless, it is an entertaining mine of information. Other Romans wrote about their own slaves sometimes, and one or two of the slaves of such writers as Cicero, the Younger Pliny and Horace become living people to us. Roman pamphlets and handbooks about agriculture often deal with agricultural slaves, and slaves play some part in Roman history too, as will become clear in later chapters. Finally, one of Rome's most lasting monuments is her legal code, and this has much to say about the legal position of slaves, though much of it refers to periods later than AD 200.

# CHAPTER ONE

# How did you become a slave?

At most periods of ancient history, and over the whole of the Mediterranean world, the most usual way of becoming a slave was to be captured in war. The Greeks got nearly all their slaves that way, usually from their barbarian neighbours, and so did the Romans, especially in the last two centuries BC, which was the peak period for acquiring slaves. During the next two centuries, being born into slavery was at least as common.

You might be captured on the field of battle, or running away from it, or in a town or city that had surrendered or been overrun. In either

1 *This slave chain for six people, nearly 4 metres (13 feet) long, was found near Cambridge. The large holes are for the slaves' necks.*

2 *The scene on this tombstone shows a slave standing on an auction block being sold.*

3 *The tombstone of Timotheos. The top part shows a funeral banquet, the middle part men at work, and the bottom part has eight slaves chained at the neck, being led along, perhaps by Timotheos himself. The inscription reads: 'Aulos Kapreilios Timotheos, freedman of Aulos, slave-dealer.' The stone was found at Amphipolis, in the north of Greece.*

case, you would soon be sold to one of the slave-dealers who followed the army at a safe distance, and he in turn would sell you wherever he could get the best price for you. Quite possibly he would take you, with all his other slaves, to Athens, and put you in the auction sale that took place in the market-place. In Roman times you might all go to Rome, or to Delos if you were captured in the eastern Mediterranean. You would be put up on a revolving platform, with a placard round your neck giving information about you, and if you had just come from abroad and were being sold for the first time both your feet would be whitened with chalk. It was customary for the seller to guarantee that the slave was healthy, not stolen but genuinely and legally owned by the seller, and not wanted by the authorities for having committed a crime. Both Athens and Rome eventually passed laws about this.

Slave-dealers were never very popular, not surprisingly, and they did not boast much about their trade. The tombstone of Aulos Kapreilios Timotheos is very unusual, because he does actually call himself a slave-trader on it, and he must have been successful, for it is an impressive monument just over 2 metres (7 feet) high. The fact that he had been a slave himself evidently did not put him off going into the trade when he was freed.

If you were not fighting in any war, you might be captured by pirates or bandits, especially if you travelled a lot. Even under the comparatively peaceful conditions of the Roman Empire, about AD 100, we still hear of travellers in Italy disappearing without trace. People always accepted this as one of the risks of travel. In early times people had not been quite sure if there was any difference between piracy and trading, and piracy was common at most periods down to the time of Augustus, the first Roman emperor (27 BC–AD 14), who did much to restore peace and prosperity to the Empire, and made travelling safer. If you were wealthy or influential, you would be more likely to be set free on payment of a large ransom, as happened to Julius Caesar in his youth. He was only twenty-five when he was captured off the coast of Asia Minor, and he was only a private citizen, but when the pirates demanded a ransom of twenty talents he laughed, and offered fifty. His friends went off to raise the money. Caesar was quite at ease with the pirates, ordering them about as if they were the prisoners and he had captured them. In forty days his friends returned with the fifty talents, and he was set free. He got together a fleet, attacked the pirates, and captured and crucified them all. They thought he had been joking when he had told them he would do just that.

If your parents did not want you when you were born, they might

4 *This vase shows hoplites – Greek infantry – in action, with their typical shields and thrusting spears. A boy plays a double flute to keep them in step as they march into battle.*

5 *This temple, the Erechtheion, was built on the Acropolis at the end of the fifth century* BC. *It is unusual because it has three 'porches' instead of being surrounded by columns. (See J. Sharwood Smith's* Temples, Priests and Worship *in this series.)*

abandon you in some lonely spot to die, and you might then be found and sold into slavery. They might even sell you to a slave-dealer themselves, as Thracians and Phrygians quite commonly did, or, even if you were wanted, you might be kidnapped and sold.

But you didn't always become a slave by violent means. If your parents were slaves (or only your mother in Roman times) then so were you, and their owner was your owner. Athenians did not often keep slave children, because they were not on the whole as wealthy as the Romans were later, and it was uneconomic. Whether they sold them or simply abandoned them we do not know for sure. At Rome, though, under the emperors, this became the commonest way of getting slaves, especially as there were fewer wars to provide them. They were often brought up with the master's children, and could thus be trained more effectively to be loyal and obedient.

Other ways of becoming a slave were less common. If you borrowed some money and could not repay it, then you were liable to become the property of your creditor. Although this remained a possibility in some Greek states it was made illegal in Athens in 594 BC, and in Rome too at a fairly early stage. You could be sold into slavery if you

6 *This is the tombstone of Regina, a girl from Essex who was bought by a Syrian soldier serving in Britain. He freed her and married her, and when she died at the age of thirty he set up this large monument to her at South Shields.*

7  *Trimalchio giving a banquet. A scene from Fellini's film of the* Satyricon.

committed certain serious crimes, but this did not happen very often. Romans sometimes condemned such criminals to work in the mines, or to fight as gladiators. Some people in the Roman Empire, if they were not Roman citizens, may have sold themselves into slavery to a Roman master, in the hope of eventually being freed and becoming Roman citizens. One of Trimalchio's guests in Petronius' *Satyricon* said he did this, but perhaps it did not happen very often in real life.

HOW MUCH DID SLAVES COST?
*Greece*
Slaves varied enormously in cost, according to how educated, skilled or beautiful they were. The tables below give some of the prices that are known, and also some prices of other things and some daily rates of pay, in order to give an idea of the value of money.

(1) *Greek money values*
6,000 drachmai = 1 talent
6 obols        = 1 drachma

## (2) *Greek rates of pay (end of fifth century BC)*

| | |
|---|---|
| Hoplite on campaign | 1 drachma per day |
| Rowers in navy | 4 obols–1 drachma per day |
| Labourers and craftsmen working on Erechtheion | 1 drachma per day |
| Jury service (expenses) | 3 obols per day |

## (3) *Greek prices*

| | |
|---|---|
| Bare minimum to live on | 3 obols per person per day |
| A sheep | 10–20 drachmai |
| An ox for ploughing | 50–100 drachmai |
| A year's wheat for 1 man | 15 drachmai |

## (4) *Cost (in drachmai) of Greek slaves sold by auction in 414 BC*

| | | |
|---|---|---|
| Small boy | 72 | |
| Females | 106 | |
| | 135 | |
| | 165 | Total: 796 drachmai |
| | 170 | Average cost: 159 drachmai |
| | 220 | |
| Males | 105 | |
| | 115 | |
| | 121 | |
| | 144 | |
| | 153 | Total: 1,684 drachmai |
| | 161 | Average cost: 168.4 drachmai |
| | 170 | |
| | 174 | |
| | 240 | |
| | 301 | |

The prices of these slaves are probably typical, but one very wealthy Athenian, called Nikias, who had more slaves than any other Greek we know about, is said to have paid one talent for the Thracian slave who managed his mining interests. He must have been very capable, if the story is true.

### Rome

If you compare Tables 2 and 3 below, you will get some idea of the gap between rich and poor at Rome. You should bear in mind that legionary soldiers were quite well paid, compared with most of the poor; and that the figure given for senators and *equites* (knights) are minimum amounts – most senators and *equites* were much wealthier.

(1) *Roman money values*
4 sestertii = 1 denarius

(2) *Roman rates of pay (in sestertii per annum)*

| Legionary | before 50 BC | 450 |
|---|---|---|
| | 50 BC–AD 83 | 900 |
| | after AD 83 | 1,200 |
| | by AD 220 | 3,000 |

(3) *Roman property qualifications*

| Senators | 1,000,000 sestertii |
|---|---|
| *Equites* | 400,000 sestertii |

(4) *Some prices of Roman slaves (in sestertii)*

| | | |
|---|---|---|
| Average for unskilled slave | second century BC | 300–600 |
| | first century AD | 2,000 |
| Cheap price for an educated young slave | 20 BC | 8,000 |
| A very learned slave | 20 BC | 700,000 |
| 2 young pages for Cleopatra | 35 BC | 100,000 each |

Unfortunately we know very little about the price of slaves during the second century BC, when they were at their cheapest. The figure in the table is a reasonable guess.

# CHAPTER TWO

# How could you stop being a slave?

Liberty was much easier to achieve if your master was Roman than if he was Greek, for Greeks, even Athenians, were not generous about freeing their slaves.

You could, of course, try running away, and sometimes quite a lot of slaves did. When Sparta was at war with Athens and established a fortress on Athenian territory in 413 BC, 20,000 slaves ran away to it. But they probably did not get their freedom, for they seem to have been sold again, mostly to Greeks from Thebes, a city not far from Athens, whose people had always hated the Athenians. There was not much point in running away in peacetime, because you were most likely a foreigner in Greece, and the chances of being recaptured were quite high. If you were caught the punishment was savage; at the very least you would be branded with hot irons, and after that everyone would know that you had run away. Even if you remained at liberty, you would have lost the security of having food, home and clothing provided for you, and you probably had little or no money or means of getting it.

In Roman times you probably had a better chance of success, simply because there was more room to hide in the Roman Empire, and more people to hide among. The same savage punishments awaited you if caught, and the laws helped the owner too. He could offer a reward, and have anyone punished who helped to hide a runaway. Later on he even got the right to enter buildings and search for his slave. There is such an incident in the *Satyricon*:

> Into the pub came a town crier with a public slave and a small crowd of other people, and shaking a torch which made more smoke than light, he made this announcement: 'A slave has just run away at the public baths; age about 16, curly hair, attractive and girlish-looking, name of Giton. A reward of 1,000 sestertii will be given to anyone who is willing to give him back or indicate his whereabouts.'
> Petronius, *Satyricon* 97

8 *This is how Fellini saw the pub where they searched for Giton, in his film of the* Satyricon.

All the rooms in the house are searched, including guest rooms. One of the doors even has to be broken down with an axe.

Sometimes slaves felt there was safety in numbers, and there were full-scale rebellions. We know about two that took place in Sicily towards the end of the second century BC, and the famous revolt of Spartacus, which lasted two years. Spartacus was a Thracian gladiator, who led a breakout of gladiators from Capua, near Naples, in 73 BC. More gladiators and other slaves quickly joined him from all over southern Italy, and he may have had as many as 90,000 followers. The rebels defeated several Roman armies, rampaged all over Italy and might even have escaped north of the Alps out of the Roman Empire altogether, had Spartacus been able to persuade them to follow him. They preferred to plunder Italy, however, and in the end the millionaire Marcus Crassus, who did not consider anyone to be rich unless he could pay a legion out of his own pocket, penned them in the south of Italy, with the help of a large army, and defeated and killed many of them in battle. Six or seven thousand of the survivors were crucified along the Appian Way leading out of Rome, to deter any other slaves who might be tempted to try to imitate Spartacus.

But slave revolts were not frequent. (They were caused by the Roman practice, common in the last two centuries BC, of having huge farms, called *latifundia*, which were owned by wealthy Romans who seldom visited them, and run by large gangs of slaves. These were very tough and were badly treated, often being kept in chains.) In times of crisis it was possible for slaves to earn their freedom quite legally by fighting. Two or three occasions are known when Athens promised freedom to slaves who fought in her defence, the most famous being in a crucial sea battle off the Arginusae Islands shortly before the end of the long war against Sparta. Athens won the battle, and the slaves who survived were freed. Rome also occasionally enlisted slaves, for instance in the dark days after the disastrous defeat by Hannibal at Cannae in 216 BC, when two legions of slaves were first freed and then enrolled in the army.

But these were not the likeliest ways for you to gain freedom. It was customary for masters to allow slaves to earn wages and keep them, and these slaves saved up to 'buy' their freedom. There was no legal backing for this: in the eyes of the law a slave was not a person, and therefore could not own anything. Still, masters often used to allow it, for it was another way to make money out of their slaves, and in Roman times replacements were not hard to come by. When the price of slaves did rise, under the Roman emperors, masters often used to insist on slaves' producing children before they bought their own freedom, so that the replacements cost nothing except their upbringing and keep.

Greeks did not always free their slaves, but when they did it was most commonly through this kind of purchase. The slave would give the money to a third person, who acted as witness, and who 'bought' the slave from his master and immediately freed him. That way there was no possibility of dispute about what had happened. Sometimes,

9 *Augustus, the first emperor
of Rome (27 BC–AD 14), who
won sole power in the civil
wars that ended the Republic.
He set up a new system of
government and did much to
restore Rome's greatness.*

but not very often, a master might free his slaves, or some of them,
simply by making a statement in his will, or a public announcement in
a theatre or law court. In some cities there was a religious ceremony
outside a temple, and the action was recorded on the wall of the
sanctuary.

Romans freed their slaves much more frequently than Greeks,
especially if they were well behaved, and were hard-working farmers
or civilised 'town' slaves. In early times there were complicated forms
to be gone through. Freeing 'by the rod' (*per vindictam*) involved a
'trial' before the *praetor* (presiding magistrate) or some other Roman
official. The slave had an 'advocate' (*assertor*) who claimed that he
was a free man, and the master did not deny it. The official touched
the slave's head with a rod to indicate that he was free – that is why the
process was called 'freeing by the rod'. A master could also free his
slave by entering his name on the censor's list of citizens, for a Roman
citizen could not be a slave; or by a declaration in his will. As time
passed, other less formal methods became popular: the master simply
stated, among his friends, that the slave was free, or wrote the slave a
letter saying so, or even just invited him to join him at dinner.
Slaves, of course, did not dine with free Romans, so if the master
invited him to do so, that was as good as saying he was free. There
would be other friends of the master at dinner too, so once again there

would be witnesses to what had happened.

So many slaves were captured in war by Rome in the last two centuries BC, and then in many cases freed, that the Emperor Augustus became worried about the effects on the Roman people of having so many citizens who were ex-slaves. By most of the methods described above slaves were freed individually, but large numbers were often freed by will, so Augustus limited the numbers and set minimum ages both for slave and master. By the age of twenty a slave's character was thought to be fully developed, but the master had to be thirty before he was considered capable of judging whether the slave would make a good citizen. This action did not do much to reverse the trend, though, and by the end of the first century AD, if not before, the great majority of the population of Rome and Italy had at least some ancestors who had been slaves. A bitter Roman satirist even wrote, 'For years now the Syrian river Orontes has poured its sewage into the Tiber in Rome', and went on to talk about the Oriental languages, customs and music which he thought had ruined the old Roman national character.

CHAPTER THREE

# What was your status when freed?

You might think that when you stopped being a slave you were free, and that was that. You would be wrong. The Greeks thought there were four main elements in complete freedom, and when you were freed you might not be given all of them. First, you became legally a person, instead of a thing. You gained the protection of the law, but you were also subject to its restrictions and could be held responsible for your own actions. In other words, you were legally your own master. Second, no one could lay hands on you, except of course in self-defence, or if you broke the law. Third, you could do what you wanted to, instead of being at someone else's beck and call, and fourth, you could go where you liked, and live and work where you liked, instead of having to go where you were told.

Since the Romans freed far more slaves than the Greeks, they naturally had more complicated and varied rules about the consequences. In Greek cities your status was the same as if you had been an alien resident in that city; you did not become a citizen of it, with the rights and duties of citizens. If you wanted to go to law, you needed a citizen to represent you, and naturally your ex-master did so. In certain rare cases, if you then gave valuable help to your adopted city, it might reward you with the precious gift of citizenship, but that was not very common. Most freedmen, at any rate in Athens, continued with the trade they had performed as slaves for their masters. Since the mark of a citizen was owning land, which an alien could not do, most citizens worked on the land, and left banking, trading and quite a lot of manufacturing to freedmen and other aliens. In fact, your master might set you free only on certain conditions, such as that you did a certain number of days' work each year for him. In this way he retained a good deal of the profits of your labour, without the bother of having to feed, clothe and house you. Better still, from his point of view, if you then died childless, he inherited all your property.

10 *Marcus Tullius Cicero (106–43 BC), Roman senator and author, the greatest Roman prose writer. He published his speeches, wrote books on philosophy and politics, and wrote countless letters, of which we still have about a thousand.*

Romans had a very strongly developed sense of mutual obligation; if a Roman performed an act of kindness for someone, he expected it to be repaid. This attitude is reflected in laws and customs about freed slaves, for they always remained to some extent under the control of their ex-master. The master who freed you became your patron (*patronus*) and you became his dependant (*cliens*). As far as the state was concerned, you were a Roman citizen ex-slave (*civis Romanus libertinus*). As a Roman citizen you had to have three names: a *nomen* to show what clan you belonged to, a *cognomen* after it to show which branch of the clan, and a *praenomen* before it for your own family to call you by. As a slave you had only one name, and you either took that as your *cognomen*, or were given a new one. Your *nomen* and *praenomen* were usually your ex-master's. For example, when Marcus Tullius Cicero freed his slave secretary, Tiro, of whom he was very fond, Tiro became a Roman citizen and was known as Marcus Tullius Tiro.

There were a number of other legal restrictions on you after you were freed. You were not allowed to serve in the Roman legions (though your sons could), but you could serve in the auxiliary forces. These were an important part of the Roman army. They were made up of units of soldiers from the provinces of the Empire, who often fought in their own traditional way, as cavalry, archers, etc. You could not be a Roman senator, nor, if you were a woman, could you marry one. You could not be a Roman knight, either, unless the Emperor said so, and he didn't very often. You could not become a magistrate in your home town, but under the emperors freedmen often became 'priests of Augustus' and played a leading part in the worship of the emperor.

These were the consequences if you were freed in the formal ways described in the last chapter; but if you were only freed informally, by letter, by invitation to dinner, or by declaration among friends, the law did not officially recognise you as free at all. You were not a Roman citizen, you were not given three names, and neither were your children. Your master, on the other hand, did not pay the tax that was levied when slaves were freed, which was 5 per cent of your cost, and no doubt that was one powerful reason why informal freeing became popular. As it did so, large numbers of these informally freed people found themselves in the awkward position of being 'non-persons', which was one of the many problems Augustus attempted to solve. He confirmed their freedom and their children's freedom, and although he would not make them Roman citizens, he did give them Latin citizenship. This was the next best thing, since it gave them some of the advantages of Roman citizens.

As a dependant of your patron, you were not what we would call free at all. Where work was concerned, the main difference between slaves and free men was that free men were self-employed, and would not take permanent paid employment under the orders of another man if they could help it. If you were a freedman, you would do so quite happily, and your ex-master, as well as becoming your patron, might also become your employer. Alternatively, as in Greece, you might have to do a certain number of days' work each year for him, or else pay him a lump sum of money for the privilege of not having to do so. It is not surprising, then, that Roman writers often refer to freedmen as slaves, and that many Romans felt a snobbish contempt for them. The poet Horace, for example, complains bitterly about a freedman who actually got into a legion as an officer, although Horace's own father was a freed slave.

You were required to serve your patron in other ways too. Together with the other dependants, not all of whom would be freedmen, you called on your patron every day at dawn to pay your respects and see if there were any little jobs to be done or favours to be gained. You could not prosecute your patron, unless the *praetor* gave you permission to do so, but you could be punished by your patron if you refused to obey his reasonable orders. If you died childless, your patron inherited your property, and if you were rich and your patron fell into poverty, you were required to support him. The obligations worked both ways, however, for a rich patron was expected to help his poor dependants, and was expected not to prosecute them. There was no Welfare State in Rome, no National Health Service, no National Insurance or Unemployment Benefit, but this system of *clientela*, whereby patron and dependant helped each other, went some way towards relieving the misery that many poor men must have suffered, even if there were individuals who abused the system or did not fulfil their obligations.

# CHAPTER FOUR

# What jobs did you do as a slave in Greece?

There were hardly any activities in Greece that we do not find both slaves and free men carrying on at some time. There were some things that only citizens could do, such as holding public office, attending meetings of the city's governing Assembly, or sitting on juries, but these activities were forbidden to all non-citizens, whether slave or free. We often hear of slaves and free men working together – in building, pottery and farming, for instance. Mining was particularly hard work and extremely dangerous, but even here we do occasionally find a free man working his own claim, though the vast majority of miners were slaves.

As is so often the case, most of our information comes from Athens, which was an unusual city in many ways. If you were a slave there, you were most likely to have been bought by your master as an

11 *The Acropolis, a rocky hill in the middle of Athens, on which parts of the Parthenon, the Erechtheion and other famous temples and buildings can still be seen.*

investment. Xenophon, an aristo-cratic army officer who wrote many books on all kinds of subjects, describes a conversation in which Socrates is trying to find out how a woman called Theodote earns her living. She has not got a farm, she says, or a house that brings in rent. Then she must own some slaves who work at a craft, says Socrates. When she denies this as well he cannot think of any other possi-bilities, and confesses himself beaten. (In fact, he knew all the time that she lived off her various boy-friends.) Wealthy Athenians might have a large number of slaves. The rich Athenian Nikias, for ex-ample, is said to have owned 1,000, whom he hired out for one obol a day each to a man who fed them and put them down the silver mines at Laureion, agreeing to replace the casualties. All Nikias had to do was sit back and accept his ten talents a year. He didn't even have to keep his accounts, for he had a very expensive slave who did that for him.

Nikias was unusual, and we do not know of anyone else who owned so many. Two other rich Athenians are said to have had 600 and 300 respectively, but much commoner was the position of a man called Timarchos, who owned nine or ten slaves. They were shoemakers who sold their own products, and the foreman paid Timarchos three obols a day, while the other slaves gave him two obols, and were allowed to keep whatever they could earn on top of that. Another man had

12 *Socrates, the Athenian philosopher, who spent most of his time questioning people to try to find out how one ought to live, and what ideals were logical and reasonable.*

13 *This vase shows us how a shoe-maker, who might well be a slave, goes about his job. The boy is accompanied by his paidagogos, also a slave (see p. 35).*

only one slave, who worked in the silver mines at Laureion, like the 1,000 owned by Nikias. We hear about him because he gave evidence about a crime which he saw being committed in the middle of the night: at the time he was walking to Laureion, thirty-five miles away, to collect his slave's wages. Not all these investment slaves were miners or shoemakers. Among the slaves sold at one auction in 414 BC (see p. 19) we find a goldsmith, a cobbler, a fabric maker, a donkey driver and a spit maker (very necessary when meat was usually roasted over an open fire).

When the Erechtheion was being built on the Acropolis in Athens, slaves, aliens and free men worked alongside each other as labourers and sculptors. All the sculptors got the same wage, one drachma per day, but whereas the free man kept his, the slave handed most of his over to his master. If you were not a craftsman, you might be good at figures, in which case you might be given a responsible job as a steward or manager. An Athenian called Archestratos owned such a

14 *The accounts the Athenians kept of the cost of building the Erechtheion. They show that slaves, aliens and citizens worked together for the same pay.*

slave, called Pasion, who managed Archestratos' bank so efficiently and honestly that it was extremely successful. The grateful Archestratos gave Pasion his freedom and, because his own sons were incompetent, actually left him the bank in his will. In fact Pasion's was a complete success story: he became one of the richest men in Athens, helped his city in a time of crisis, and was rewarded with the rare gift of citizenship. In his old age he leased the bank to a slave of his own, Phormio, who was also freed and became wealthy.

Such success was possible for able slaves, because Athenian citizens would not accept permanent paid employment where they had to take orders, and if they wanted to employ a manager, they preferred to have someone they could legally punish if he was incom-

15  *A cup showing a school scene at Athens. Boys are learning poetry, the lyre and the double flute. The men leaning on sticks are* paidagogoi *(see p. 35).*

petent or dishonest. Another of the conversations of Socrates recorded by Xenophon was with a man called Eutheros, who was short of money. When Socrates advised him to get a job, Eutheros said he would find it hard to give up his freedom, because in principle he had no wish to be responsible to anybody. He preferred to hire himself out for a limited period, even if it was for manual work, than to take a job for an unlimited time.

What if you were not a skilled craftsman or a capable manager? If you were sturdy enough, you might be an agricultural slave,

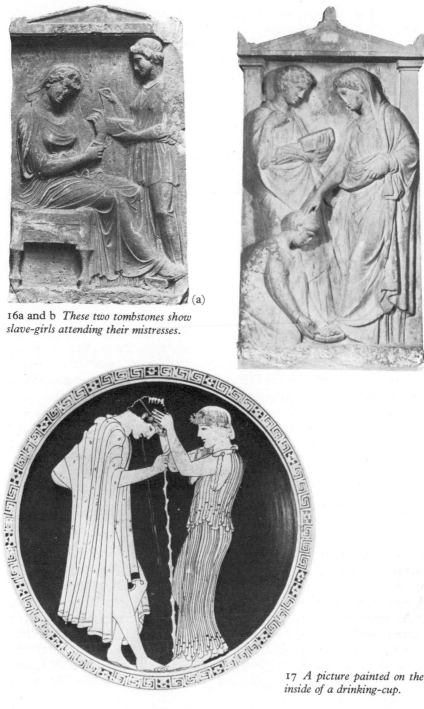

16a and b *These two tombstones show slave-girls attending their mistresses.*

(a)

(b)

17 *A picture painted on the inside of a drinking-cup.*

though there do not seem to have been as many of these as we might expect considering that the Greek city states were largely agricultural. A peasant farmer might be able to afford a slave to help him with the hard work, but it did mean another mouth to feed. There were not many wealthy landowners in Greece, and their estates would not be very extensive, either, compared with those of the Romans, but the farms would probably be run and worked mostly by slaves, with perhaps a few tenant farmers. They would probably have some personal and domestic slaves too, but not more than a dozen or so, even in the richest households, for the Greeks were not much given to luxury in their private lives.

You might be employed as a *paidagogos* to look after a rich man's son and take him to school, to keep him in order there and bring him home again. If you were educated you might even teach the boy, but then you would have been a very expensive slave, and only a very rich man could have afforded to buy you. If he was extravagant he might also buy a slave who was a jester, juggler or acrobat to entertain the guests at his dinner parties, and perhaps to be hired out to his friends for theirs.

So far we have only dealt with slaves bought by private individuals, but the state bought slaves too. One of the strangest things about Athenian society is that its policemen were slaves, the so-called 'Scythian Archers'. Although they were armed, and could arrest citizens, they were nothing like as powerful as police forces nowadays, partly because they were strictly controlled by elected officials, who would of course be Athenian citizens, and partly because in many cases it was up to the victim and his family to arrest and prosecute the criminal. In one of Aristophanes' comedies the Archers are sent out into the market-place and streets to round up citizens and bring them to a meeting of the city's Assembly (they were liable to be fined if they shirked it). In another play one of the Archers is told to guard a slippery prisoner for a short while. Being an ignorant foreigner he lets the man get away.

The state employed slaves in a variety of other capacities – as road-menders and sweepers, as workers in the state Mint, and as clerks to some public officials. The public executioner was a slave, and so were the heralds who made announcements at public meetings. A very important slave was the secretary who sat behind the president at Assembly meetings, which were held four times a month. He might be required to produce the text of any decree or law at short notice, so he needed to know his job very well. In 410 BC the Athenians decided to reorganise the city's laws completely, and Nicomachos, who was secretary at the time, was given the job of revising them and

18 a *Statuette of a dancing-girl.*
   b *Girl playing a double-flute.*

drawing up a new code. Later he was freed and given the citizenship.

You might not be a man at all, of course. Women were enslaved too. They had two main functions. Either they assisted the lady of the house with her spinning and weaving, waiting on her, or looking after her children; or else they provided entertainment for the men. Instead of having a jester, juggler or acrobat, the master of the house might prefer to entertain his guests with flute-girls or dancing-girls, especially if they were pretty. Not surprisingly, they were a popular subject for vase painters, who sometimes liked to show people enjoying themselves. If the master of the house were more economical in his tastes, and wanted value for money, he might prefer to buy a housekeeper. Xenophon gives good advice on how to choose one. You should pick out 'the woman who seems least inclined to gluttony, drink, sleep and running after men; she must also have an excellent memory, and she must be capable of either foreseeing the punishment which neglect will cost her, or of thinking of ways of pleasing her masters and deserving their favour.'

Not all women slaves were unproductive. Timarchos, who owned the shoemakers (see p. 31), also had a skilled female weaver, whose work was sold to increase her master's profits. And yet another of Xenophon's conversations tells us that several rich Athenians lived off the labour of female slaves. Socrates is talking to a man called Aristarchos, who has fourteen female relatives to feed and is at his wits' end. Socrates suggests setting them to work making clothes and baking, so that Aristarchos can sell their products. He goes on to name several Athenians who do sell such things, but Aristarchos points out that they buy slaves who do the work. He himself is an aristocrat, and it is unthinkable for his family to do such humble work.

It has been claimed that the slave system was harmful in its effects on the Greeks. It has been suggested as a reason why they never turned their undoubted scientific skill towards inventing labour-saving machines, and this may be partly true, though many other factors are involved too. It has also been said that slave labour made things worse for poor free men, because it deprived them of work. This seems unlikely, for when slave and free worked on the same job they received the same wages, and there was therefore no reason for anyone to prefer to employ the slave. Where manufacturing was concerned, a buyer had to be found for the finished article, and the slave had to charge enough to pay for his own keep and his master's profit; so there was little chance of his undercutting the price of a free man's product. In fact, most Athenian citizens were peasant farmers, who sold their small amount of surplus produce at market, using the proceeds to buy the few articles they could not make for themselves. So it is likely that a good deal of what these manufacturing slaves produced was bought either for other slaves, or by the large number of aliens resident in Athens, or, in the case of luxury goods, by the wealthy slave-owning class itself.

CHAPTER FIVE

# What jobs did you do as a slave in Rome?

The Romans conquered more territories than the Greeks, so they captured more prisoners. That meant they had more slaves, and so they gave them a very wide variety of jobs to do. As a Roman slave, just like a Greek slave, you might find yourself doing almost anything, except for the things that only citizens could do. You would not vote in any of the governing Assemblies, hold public office, serve on juries or fight in the army, except on the rare occasions of crisis described in Chapter Two (see p. 23). You would not row in the Emperor's fleet, either, for that was done by free provincials, but oddly enough, if you were one of the Emperor's slaves, you might be a ship's captain.

Mines and quarries were owned by the state, so there would be no reason for free men to work in them. Mining is a dangerous enough business now, but in ancient times it was much more dangerous, and since you were not very valuable as a slave, and not very expensive to replace, hardly any research was done to make it safer. We think of coal as the main product of mines, but the Romans had not discovered its use as a source of power, and were much more concerned with metals. Silver and gold were precious, and iron, tin, copper and lead were useful.

Almost as dangerous was your life as a gladiator, for the Romans found it more and more entertaining to watch people killing each other, especially if they put up a good fight first. There were some compensations here, though, with the result that sometimes free men volunteered to fight as gladiators, and even one of the emperors, Commodus, fancied himself as one. The living conditions were hard, of course, and training was tough, but if you were a consistent winner you might be allowed to retire undefeated, with the respect of the men and the admiration of the girls. The Romans seem to have picked up the habit of holding gladiatorial contests quite early in their history, from their Etruscan neighbours, who put on fights between gladiators at the funerals of the kings. While the Romans were busy building up

19a and b *Gladiators were a popular subject in art. This is a mosaic floor from a rich man's villa in Italy.*

20 *An exciting moment in the chariot race in the film* Ben Hur.

their Empire, gladiatorial contests did not take place all that often, but towards the end of the Republic and under the first emperors the number of gladiators increased sharply. Julius Caesar, in a bid for popularity early in his career, put on a show with 320 pairs of gladiators in 65 BC; Augustus built the first permanent amphitheatre in Rome and put on 5,000 fights altogether during his long reign. The emperors Vespasian and Titus built the famous Colosseum, which held 50,000 spectators, and put on exhibitions for a hundred days to celebrate its opening; and in AD 107 the Emperor Trajan equalled Augustus' 5,000 fights in only four months. By this time gladiatorial fights were almost as popular as chariot races, although some of the more civilised Romans, including Cicero, Pliny and the Emperor Tiberius, said they disliked them.

If you worked on one of the huge farms, or *latifundia*, which wealthy Romans owned but seldom visited, your life would not be so dangerous, but you would need to be tough. You might have to defend your master's flocks and herds, and yourself, against bandits, wolves and even lions. You had nowhere to run away to, unless some Spartacus happened to come round looking for more slaves to swell his rebel mob, and you would probably be kept in chains anyway – though Pliny, in a letter to a friend, declared that he never kept his slaves in chains, whatever other people might do. These farms grew up after the war against Hannibal when land became very cheap. Much of Italy, especially the south, had been devastated by Hannibal, and was therefore less valuable, and many of the peasants who had previously farmed it were now soldiers. Slaves became cheap then,

21 *The Colosseum in Rome.*

too, so although it was not a very efficient method of farming, it was not at all expensive.

In the fertile parts of Italy, you would be more likely to work at a country farmhouse (*villa rustica*). Your master might own one or several of these, as well as a town house, if he was a senator or wealthy knight, and if you worked hard and earned his favour you might be promoted to work in the town house. On the farm, as well as the labourers who did the ploughing, sowing, harvesting and all the other necessary jobs, there would be slaves to provide for their needs, to prepare their food, make their clothes, cut their hair, and try to cure them if they fell ill. There would be a slave in charge of the labourers, and a slave steward (*vilicus*) to manage the whole farm. He would be helped by his wife, also a slave, and perhaps by an accountant (*actor*) to keep the books, unless he could find time to do them himself. The steward and accountant might expect to gain their freedom if they worked hard and were honest, and they might be on quite good terms with their master. Horace wrote a poem in the form of a friendly letter to his steward, in which he longs for the peace and quiet of his farm, while he imagines the steward grumbling at the boredom of the countryside and longing for the pleasures of the city.

The 'town household' (*familia urbana*) might be large or small, according to how rich the master was. There were names for the jobs of a large number of different slaves, but we should not imagine that many people had all of them. Most of the houses that have been excavated, even those of wealthy Romans, are not big enough to have held a large number of slaves. But in a very wealthy and luxurious house, there might be slaves who were cooks, and other kitchen staff, under the control of a head cook; waiters to serve at table, attendants to assist the master and his wife to wash and dress, to wash and iron clothes, to heat water and prepare the baths, to trim the lamps and light them,

22 *A negro musician. He probably held a lyre in his hands, and was using it to accompany his song.*

to clean the house and its furniture, to look after and perhaps to
teach the children, and generally to act as labour-saving machines
in a hundred and one different ways – for that after all is exactly
what they were. Such a wealthy man would be likely to own singers,
dancers and musicians to entertain his guests; litter bearers to carry
him and his family when they went out; athletics trainers and
masseurs to keep him more or less fit; or if he was a literary type,
like Cicero and his friend Atticus, there would be clerks, secretaries,
copyists, shorthand writers and librarians to administer his library
and deal with his correspondence, and runners to deliver the letters.
He would certainly have a *dispensator* to keep his accounts, and
quite possibly other slaves to be in charge of the money and produce
it when necessary. All these slaves would be under the control
of a *procurator*, who would have to be a very responsible and trust-
worthy slave, or perhaps a freedman. If you rose to a position like
that you would be a very powerful person, and could almost certainly
look forward to gaining your freedom and Roman citizenship
when your master died, if not before. When you did gain your
freedom you would be quite rich, too, like Trimalchio in the *Satyricon*:
he had been a *dispensator*, and in the novel he owns more than 400
slaves himself, organised into squads of ten, each under its own leader.
He might even have bought some of the slaves before he was freed,
for that was quite often allowed.

23  *A scene from Trimalchio's banquet in Fellini's film of the* Satyricon.

24 *A little statue of a slave-boy who has been lighting the way for his master, perhaps when he went out to dinner, and is now waiting to escort him home again.*

Leading Romans thought it important to make an impressive show in public, so when they went down to the Forum on business they liked to be accompanied by crowds of dependants and slaves. On less formal occasions they might only take one or two slaves out. One of these had the important job of reminding his master of the name of anyone they happened to meet in the street, so that the master could greet him by name. Some slaves would also be needed to attend the master or mistress if they went to the public baths, which became a popular meeting-place and centre of gossip.

Like the Athenians, the Romans used to hire out the labour of their slaves and sell their products, though not perhaps to the same extent. These slaves were often allowed to set up their own workshops, away from the master's house, just as they sometimes were in Athens. They would keep their own accounts, and would presumably have them checked at regular intervals – say once a month – by the master or his *procurator*, who would collect the agreed amount from the slave. They might not be productive slaves at all: one of Trimalchio's guests, for example, had a slave friend who kept an inn. Or they might belong to what we should call the professional classes. The wealthy Marcus Crassus is said to have made some of his money by buying slave architects and builders, and then buying houses that were either burning themselves or in the path of others that were burning. Fires were frequent among the ramshackle houses of Ancient Rome, and their owners, in such a crisis, would be only too anxious to get any price they could for the doomed houses. So Crassus would buy them cheaply, rebuild at little expense, and sell again at a great profit. He also organised slaves into a fire service to put the flames out – after he had bought the houses, of course. We are not told whether he organised slaves to light the fires as well.

As in Athens, you might be a public slave. Under the amateurish

25 *An outstanding example of a Roman aqueduct: the Pont du Gard in the south of France.*

system of the Republic there were not many of these, for the important officials were elected Roman citizens, and if they needed any secretarial work done they often used their own slaves. But running a large empire was more complicated, and Rome began to buy public slaves for officials to use. The growth of the city's water supply system

26 *Marcus Vipsanius Agrippa, Augustus' great general, who later married his daughter Julia.*

27 *Slave sitting on an altar.*

28 *A scene in a shop. The two customers, who are seated, are citizens. Any or all of the others may be slaves, even the salesman standing in the middle, who may be the owner of the shop.*

is a good illustration of this development. At first it was the job of the censors to have aqueducts built, and of the aediles to keep them maintained. They were not very efficient about it, and in 33 BC Augustus' friend Agrippa took up the aedileship, though it was a minor post much beneath his dignity. He had two more aqueducts built and trained 240 of his own slaves to maintain all of them. When he died, he bequeathed the slaves to Augustus, who built two more aqueducts and presented the slaves to the state. By the time Claudius was emperor, Rome was supplied with 38 gallons of water per person per day, brought by 280 miles of aqueduct. A total of 660 public slaves was needed to maintain and administer the system, whereas a century earlier censors and aediles had made do with a handful of their own slaves.

The Imperial Civil Service which administered Rome and the Empire for the emperors was composed of slaves and freedmen belonging to the Emperor. The system developed from the 'town households' of leading senators under the Republic, but where they had had a *procurator*, a *dispensator* and a few secretaries and clerks, the Emperor was concerned with administering large areas of territory

29 *A scene in a shop. As in the illustration on page 45, the two customers sitting down are citizens. They have brought two slaves to attend them. Two slaves belonging to the shop hold up the goods for inspection, and the man on the left is probably the shop owner. He too may be a slave.*

30 *A scene in a potter's workshop, with one of the slaves being whipped.*

himself, and had a private fortune of a size that even people like Crassus never dreamed of. If you were a 'slave of Caesar', or were freed and became a 'freedman of Augustus', you could be a very powerful person indeed. You might have rich senators coming to you and begging you to use your influence with the Emperor to obtain promotion or favours for them. Free men might despise you as a slave, but they would certainly respect your power. On the other hand, of course, you might only be a very junior clerk, accountant, shorthand writer or messenger, especially if you had not been sent to one of the two training schools for Imperial slaves in Rome.

As time went by, it was not thought right that such important posts should be held by slaves and freedmen, and they were given to Roman knights (*equites*) instead, for they were the social equals of senators. Slaves in general became more expensive, since there were few major wars, and therefore fewer prisoners. As slaves became more expensive, farms were more often worked by free tenants, and more manufacturing was done by free men. In the old days, the stern old senator and writer, Cato, like other rich Romans, had bought a Greek teacher, for many Greek slaves were more cultured and educated than their Roman masters. Being a shrewd man, he had not had his own children taught by this slave, but had hired him out to other senators. Later on, however, under the emperors, teachers, like doctors and other skilled professionals, were more likely to be free-born men, although there might still be a slave *paedagogus*, as in Greece, to take the boy to school, look after him, and bring him home.

Roman society was very complex, and slaves played a large and varied part in it. The huge numbers of slaves who were brought to Italy in the second century BC from the East were used mainly as personal servants or literary assistants, for they would often be educated men, but if they came from the western half of the Empire they would be more likely to be agricultural slaves, miners or gladiators. Under the emperors, more gladiators were required, and fewer agricultural slaves. The Imperial Civil Service needed ever-increasing numbers, but the Emperor did not free his slaves until they had bred their own replacements. Indeed, most people now replaced their slaves in this way, since there were relatively few wars of conquest.

# CHAPTER SIX

# How would you be treated?

Your treatment would depend very much on your job, and on how closely you worked with your master. If you could build up a personal relationship with him your life was likely to be much easier, but even then it all depended on his nature. If he was tyrannical or vicious, you would suffer. If he was kind and generous, you would benefit.

On the whole, Greeks treated their slaves quite well – in fact better than most other ancient societies. There were exceptions, of course, notably in the silver mines at Laureion, where the Athenians kept thousands of slaves working hard for long hours underground in dangerous conditions. If you found yourself down there, you would be lucky to get out alive. Then again the Greeks, like the Romans, suffered from the strange delusion that the evidence of a slave in court was totally worthless unless the slave had been tortured first. The Romans do seem to have realised eventually that torture did not necessarily make the evidence reliable, and only used evidence obtained in this way when they had nothing else to go on. We do not know (though we can guess) what the slaves thought of this idea, but free Greeks were capable of finding amusement in the system: at any rate there is a hilarious scene in Aristophanes' comedy the *Frogs* involving evidence given under torture. The god Dionysus has taken his slave Xanthias down to Hades, to try to bring back a poet to Athens. Dionysus is a cowardly god, and whenever danger threatens he orders Xanthias to change places with him. After a while the authorities get confused and don't know which is which, so Xanthias suggests a whipping contest to settle the matter. Since Dionysus is a god, he says, he will not feel the pain, so the first one to cry out will be shown to be a slave. What he does not point out is that Dionysus certainly does feel pain, though he will not admit it, whereas Xanthias is used to being knocked about and shrugs it off. Each is struck in turn, and finds ingenious and amusing ways of pretending that his shrieks of pain do not mean he has been hurt.

Greek thinkers also turned their attention to slavery, but they did not come to the conclusion that it ought to be abolished, any more than anyone else in the ancient world, though one or two obviously felt uneasy about it. They were quite certain that Greeks were superior to barbarians, because they were free, and acknowledged only the law as their master, whereas barbarians were normally the slaves of their kings. So they came to the conclusion that barbarians were slaves by nature, and therefore it was quite all right to enslave them; but that Greeks ought not to be enslaved. Since a slave was a living machine, it seemed quite reasonable that his waking life should consist of work, food and punishment.

So much for theory: what was your life like in practice? A rather snobbish Athenian, writing at the end of the fifth century BC, seems to feel very bitter about the permissive age in which he is living. A slave won't get out of the way for you in the street, he says, and you are not allowed to strike him. There is good sense in that, he goes on, for slaves and free men dress in the same way, and you can't tell them apart. You might find you had struck a free man, and then you would be in trouble. This writer thought that the Athenians kept their slaves in the lap of luxury, so that they would not want to run away. Presumably in his younger days they were treated much more harshly, as they still were elsewhere in Greece.

If your master bought you as a house slave, you would enter his house with the same ritual as his bride did when he married, that is, you would be showered with nuts and dried fruit. (Nowadays we use confetti.) You would take part in the family's worship of the gods, and you could be initiated into the Eleusinian Mysteries, the secret worship of Demeter, the goddess of corn, which took place every year at Eleusis. In at least one Greek city you had a legal right to have your own wife and children. This was not the case at Athens, though in practice it was usually allowed.

If you were not a household slave, and your master had invested in you for your skill at some craft, you would probably be set up in a workshop somewhere else, possibly even in a different town. You would thus be almost a free man, to our way of thinking, except that your master would take a certain proportion of the money you earned, and you could not change jobs or move unless he agreed to it. If you were a public slave (see p. 35) you might be even better off, for these were sometimes allowed to live where they liked, and received their clothing and an allowance for their food. If you were economical you might save up your money and buy your freedom in only a few years. Later on there were benefit clubs which lent money to slaves to help them buy their freedom, in rather the same way that building societies nowadays help people to buy houses.

It is difficult to be sure about the day-to-day treatment of slaves, but presumably it varied according to the nature of the master. If we are to believe the playwright Aristophanes, who wrote many scenes involving slaves, they were all idle, sly rascals, whose greatest delight was in cheating and cheeking their masters and gossiping about them behind their backs. But that sort of slave is much more amusing to watch on stage than the docile, obedient, hard-working one – so much so, in fact, that the cunning slave became a stock figure in Greek comedy, was imitated by the Romans, and found his way into modern literature in the comedies of the French playwright Molière. Even if Aristophanes preferred to write mainly about one sort of slave, the relationship seems to have been a fairly free and easy one, though there was no doubt who was the master. We are reminded not so much of tyrants with whips as of teachers and children; indeed it may be significant that both Greeks and Romans called their slaves 'boy'. The slave may have been thought of as a machine, but sensible people look after their machines, even if only to make sure they go on working properly.

As a Roman slave, although you were more likely to gain your freedom, you were also more likely to be badly treated. Just as in Greece, your evidence in court could only be given after torture; and miners had a brutal and dangerous life, as we can see from this description of life in the silver mines in the province of Spain:

When Spain came into the hands of the Romans, the mines were run by a horde of Italians, whose greed made them unbelievably rich. They bought large numbers of slaves, and handed them over to the overseers in the mines. . . .

Although the slaves imprisoned in these mines make their owners fantastically rich, they work night and day in these golden prisons and many of them die there from overwork. They have no rest or break from their labour, for the overseers whip them and force them to work beyond endurance, so that in the end they die in utter misery. Some of them are sufficiently strong in body and vigorous in spirit to survive this treatment, but their lives are so wretched and their suffering so great that they would rather be dead.                                           Diodorus Siculus 5, 38

The Romans were aware of the danger of being surrounded by large numbers of badly treated slaves, and they developed the practice of executing all the slaves who lived under the same roof if their master was found murdered. There was no question of any trial, for it was felt that even if the slaves were innocent of the murder they ought to have found out that it was planned and prevented it. A Roman historian tells us of just such a case in AD 61, when an important official, Pedanius Secundus, was found murdered, and all his 400 slaves were executed. In AD 105 the Consul himself was found dead. On this occasion the Senate even discussed whether the Consul's freedmen should be executed, banished or let off, so presumably once again all the slaves were executed without question.

In the same period, Pliny wrote to one of his friends describing the murder of another important senator (*Letters* 3, 14):

This horrible affair demands more publicity than a letter – Larcius Macedo, a senator and ex-praetor, has fallen a victim to his own slaves. Admittedly he was a cruel and overbearing master, too ready to forget that his father had been a slave, or perhaps too keenly conscious of it. He was taking a bath in his house at Formiae when suddenly he found himself surrounded; one slave seized him by the throat while the others struck his face and hit him in the chest and stomach and – shocking to say – his private parts. When they thought he was dead they threw him onto the hot pavement, to make sure he was not still alive. Whether unconscious or pretending to be so, he lay there motionless, thus making them believe that he was quite dead. Only then was he carried out, as if he had fainted with the heat, and received by those of his slaves who had remained faithful, while his concubines ran up, screaming frantically. Roused by their cries and revived by the cooler air he opened his eyes and made some movement to show that he was still alive, it being now safe to do so. The guilty slaves fled, but most of them have been arrested and a search is being made for the others. Macedo was brought back to life with difficulty, but only for a few days; at least he died with the satisfaction of having revenged himself, for he lived to see the same punishment meted out as for murder. There you see the dangers, outrages, and insults to which we are exposed. No master can feel safe because he is kind and considerate; for it is their brutality, not their reasoning capacity, which leads slaves to murder masters.

But the picture is not entirely black. Just as the Greeks had their benefit clubs, Roman slaves had clubs which they called *collegia*. Here you might find yourself mixing with freedmen on equal terms, and there might be free-born men there too. They held meetings and dinners, worshipped together, and helped members to put money aside for a decent funeral, which was felt to be important.

In December, the Romans celebrated the Saturnalia, or festival of the god Saturn, from which some of our Christmas traditions are derived. One that has not survived is that you were allowed to change places with your master and give the orders while he slaved. Some cruel masters were perhaps too frightened to allow this to happen, but on one occasion the custom prevented a mutiny in the army. In AD 43 Claudius decided to invade Britain. He sent out a large force, under the command of an experienced general called Aulus Plautius, but the troops were frightened and angry at having to serve in such a place, which seemed to them like the ends of the earth, and would not obey Plautius. Claudius then sent his freedman, Narcissus, one of the most powerful men in Rome, with instructions to tell the troops off and make them follow Plautius. This made them even angrier, and the situation looked as if it was going to get out of hand, until they suddenly started calling out, 'Io Saturnalia' ('Merry Christmas', as we would say) – for here was a slave giving orders to free men. The tension was broken, and the invasion went ahead as planned.

The attitude of masters to their slaves varied, of course, and seems to have progressed over the years. Cato the Censor, writing on agriculture in the second century BC, recommended that slaves should be looked after like animals, though not as carefully as oxen, because oxen could not look after themselves. They should get plenty of food and sleep, so that they could work hard, and they should not be given any spare time, since that was wasteful. When they were too old to work any more they should be disposed of, so as not to be a drain on the resources of the household. Being rather shrewd financially, Cato used to encourage his slaves to buy other slaves and train them, and even lent them money to do so. When they were trained Cato might buy them himself, no doubt very cheaply, or if they were not what he required they would be sold at market.

This attitude strikes us as callous, but it reflects Cato's nature. A friend of Augustus once fed a careless slave, who had dropped a precious vase, to his lampreys, much to Augustus' disgust, and Galen, the famous physician, saw many slaves with black eyes and broken teeth. On the other hand, there are also indications of good treatment. Seneca, a Roman philosopher, statesman and business-man, writing in the first century AD, advised: 'Treat your slave with kindness, with courtesy too; let him share your conversations, your plans and your company.' Cicero wrote a most anxious letter to his secretary, Tiro, who had fallen ill while travelling in Greece, and some years later Cicero's son wrote Tiro a friendly letter, partly perhaps because he wanted Tiro to use his influence with his father, who was being rather difficult. When Cicero was standing for election to the consulship, many years earlier, his brother wrote advising him to see that everyone he knew supported him, even his slaves, because 'they invariably start the rumours about you that spread all over the city'.

In the long series of civil wars which threw Rome into confusion in the last century of the Republic, there were notable examples of devotion of all kinds, including that of slaves to their masters. A man called Restio was on the run.

When he fled, thinking that he was alone, he was followed secretly by a slave he had brought up himself, who had been very well treated formerly, but lately had been branded for bad conduct. While Restio was stopping in a marsh the slave came up to him. He was startled at the sight, but the slave said that he did not feel the pain of the brand so much as he remembered the kindness shown to him before. Then he found a resting-place for his master in a cave, and by working produced such food for him as he could. The soldiers in the neighbourhood had their suspicions aroused concerning Restio, and went towards the cave. The slave saw them and followed them, and seeing an old man walking in front of them, he ran up and killed him and cut off his head. The soldiers were astonished. They arrested him as a highwayman, but he said, 'I have killed Restio, my master, the man who marked me with these scars.' The soldiers took the head from him for the sake of the reward, and hurried to the city, where they discovered their mistake. The slave got his master away and took him by ship to Sicily.

Appian, *Civil War* 4, 43

CHAPTER SEVEN

# Your legal rights, and punishments

During most periods of history you had very few rights as a slave, and most of them were not intended to protect you as a person, but as part of your master's property; or else they were meant to avoid the anger of the gods which was bound to afflict the community in the case of murder, even the murder of slaves.

If you were murdered in Greece, your master was obliged by law to find out who the murderer was, and prosecute him. If the verdict was guilty, the murderer was exiled, so that the anger of the gods should fall elsewhere. If you were only injured, then your master had the right to sue for damage to his property. If he was a humane man, he might go to law on your behalf, and not just for his own sake. There is even one extreme case of a son who prosecuted his own father for the murder of a slave through neglect. In Athens, if you were badly treated by your own master, you could run for sanctuary to the temple of Theseus, but you might be jumping out of the frying-pan into the fire, for if you did go there and refused to go back you had to be sold to someone else.

Roman law, like Greek law, did not recognise you as a person if you were a slave. You were a thing, and part of your master's property; a living thing, admittedly, but still a thing. You had no legal protection against your master, and you could not marry or own property. On the other hand; we should remember that your master's son was in the same position, for in theory a father had the power of life and death over his own children. After the war against Hannibal, although the position of children improved, at any rate in practice, that of slaves got worse, for they were very numerous and therefore very cheap. You could go to court only to claim liberty on the grounds of unjust enslavement, and then you needed an *assertor* (see p. 24), and cast-iron proof, or you would be in trouble when your master got you home again.

Under the emperors laws about slaves gradually became more

humane. The Emperor Claudius decreed that if you fell ill and were abandoned and then got well again, you should be free, and in the first half of the second century AD your master finally lost his legal power of life and death over you. By the time we get to the third century, when Constantine the Great was emperor, murder of a slave and of a free man were regarded as equally serious crimes and carried the same penalties. Laws were passed enforcing what had previously only been customs. The law never actually recognised marriage between slaves, but it did say that slaves who lived together as man and wife should not be sold separately; and there were laws about your *peculium*, or property, as well. It was customary to allow slaves who earned money to keep it, as we have already seen (Chapter Two), and you could spend it on your own pleasures, or save it up to buy your freedom. Not all masters would allow you to keep your *peculium*, and even if you could it remained legally your master's property; he counted it as part of his own wealth and could take it back at any time. If you died, your master naturally did take it back, and if you swindled someone, in order to increase your *peculium*, the unfortunate victim had to sue your master; you could not be sued yourself, for you were not legally a person. But if you were so foolish as to do such a thing, your master had plenty of ways of getting his own back on you. On the other hand, especially if you were a craftsman who worked in your own workshop outside your master's household, you could not carry on your business and sell your products if you did not have control of your shop, your tools and your stock, and perhaps some slaves who worked for you. If you were sold, your *peculium* was normally sold with you, though your master would doubtless feel able to charge a higher price than if he was just selling you by yourself, without any *peculium*. If he set you free, your *peculium* became your property, after your master had taken away whatever he thought was a reasonable payment for your freedom.

At most times, your master could punish you in any way he liked, for the law did not tell him what he could or could not do with his own property. If your master was cruel and vicious, you might suffer almost any punishment, but many Greeks and Romans were either civilised or sensible, or both. A civilised man would see no point in senseless cruelty, and a sensible one would realise that it was foolish to cripple or destroy his own property. Whipping was probably the usual punishment, in both Greece and Rome, and individual masters might be able to think of interesting variations on it. If you were persistently lazy, or dishonest, or incompetent, you might be sold in the market or sent down the mines. If you ran away, you would be branded with hot irons when you were caught, and you would

31 *Inside the Colosseum. These are the passages under the floor of the arena, where wild animals were penned.*

carry the letters on your forehead for the rest of your life to indicate that you were a runaway. The Romans did the same with thieves and sometimes with liars, too.

A Roman master might demote you from town house to country farm work, or send you to work in chains at the mill-wheel, or in a hard-labour prison, until these were abolished by the Emperor Hadrian. If you had committed some serious crime, or evidence was required in a lawcourt, you might be stretched on the rack or mutilated in various ways, or, most serious of all, your legs would be broken. Finally, if you were being disposed of, you might be thrown to the wild beasts in places like the Colosseum, or wrapped in a cloak steeped in tar and burnt alive. But the most common method of execution for slaves was crucifixion. A heavy beam would be placed across your shoulders and your arms would be stretched round it and tied there. Then you would be whipped to the place of execution, hoisted up onto a vertical post and perhaps nailed to it. You would be left to die there in agony.

32  *A scene from* Ben Hur, *showing Christ carrying the beam of his cross to the place of execution.*

# CHAPTER EIGHT

# How many were there, and who owned them?

The question of the number of slaves in the ancient world is a very difficult one, which scholars have long argued about. They have approached it from both ends, first by trying to work out total numbers of slaves as compared with free men, and secondly by collecting as many examples as they could of numbers owned by known individuals.

*Known numbers of Greek slaves*

| | |
|---|---|
| Nikias | 1,000 (miners) |
| A rich Athenian | 600 (miners) |
| Another rich Athenian | 300 (miners) |
| Polemarchos and Lysias | 120 (a shield factory) |
| Demosthenes' father | 52 (32 cutlers; 20 bedmakers) |
| Kephisodoros | 16 |
| Timarchos | 10 or 11 (1 weaver, the rest shoemakers) |
| Plato | 5 (personal attendants) |

We are told that the first three figures above are exceptionally large, and the shield factory was producing shields for Athens as part of the war effort against Sparta. Demosthenes says his father's factory was a large-scale business. It seems likely, therefore, that the ten or eleven slaves owned by Timarchos represent the average number a well-to-do Athenian would invest his money in.

Plato was rich, but did not believe in having an unnecessarily large number of slaves. In the comedies of Aristophanes most of the characters, who tend to be middle class, have two or three slaves, and we may take that as normal. Thus the overall picture is that the poorest third of the population could not afford a slave at all (Aristotle said that the ox was the poor man's slave), the middle third might have two or three, while the wealthiest section of the population would have money to invest. Some would invest in land, others in slaves.

As far as total numbers are concerned, one ancient writer tells us that there were 400,000 slaves in Athens, but modern estimates put the number in 431 BC, when the slave population was at its largest, somewhere between 80,000 and 100,000, with a total free population of 200,000 to 250,000. Thus there would be two slaves to every five free people (including women and children and foreigners).

When we turn to the number of Roman slaves, the scale is quite different, as the table below shows. It gives the total number of slaves falling into Roman hands after the various wars and battles between 260 BC and 50 BC.

| | |
|---|---:|
| 1st Carthaginian war (264–241 BC) | 75,000 |
| 2nd Carthaginian war, from Tarentum alone | 30,000 |
| 3rd Macedonian war (170–167 BC) from Epirus (north-west Greece) | 150,000 |
| Invading German tribes in 102–101 BC | 150,000 |
| Caesar's conquest of Gaul, 58–50 BC | ?500,000 |

As to who owned the slaves, it is difficult to establish a clear picture. There is no doubt that the emperors owned many more slaves than anyone else, for they came to form the Civil Service which carried on a good deal of the administration of the Empire, but it is impossible to say how many of these 'slaves of Caesar' there were. We are told that some Romans owned between 10,000 and 20,000, but since this information comes from the same writer who tells us that there were 400,000 slaves at Athens, we cannot be sure that he is right. A man who died in 8 BC is known to have owned 4,116, and he claimed that he had lost a good many in the civil wars. Incidentally he was a freedman himself. We cannot tell what all his slaves were doing, though as he also possessed even greater numbers of cattle, presumably he owned *latifundia* (see p. 23), on which many of his slaves worked. Trimalchio, in the *Satyricon*, has so many in his household that they have to be divided into squads of ten, and when one slave is brought in for questioning by his master, Trimalchio does not even recognise him. He says that he is in the fortieth squad, so Trimalchio has at least 400 in the household. That was the number owned by Pedanius Secundus, the official murdered in AD 61 (see p. 51). On the other hand a man who died in AD 45, and who had been a consul, had only eight slaves. The poet Horace makes fun of the inconsistency of a man who has 'now 200 slaves, now 10', so presumably ten slaves was thought rather mean for a man who was well off. Horace's own farm was worked by eight slaves and five tenants, who were poor free men, and he claimed that he was economising without being mean by having three slaves to serve his supper. Cato, whom we met on pages 47 and 52, was always held up as an example of traditional Roman moderation and restraint, and so was his famous great-grandson, Cato of Utica. Old Cato only took three slaves with him when he went out to govern Spain, and his great-grandson had fifteen altogether when he was a junior officer in the army. We can assume that Augustus was being very reasonable when he arranged that no one going into exile should be allowed to take more than twenty slaves.

( So it appears that there was roughly one slave per Roman household. But many more Romans than Greeks were too poor to own slaves, while wealthy Romans could sometimes own very large numbers, so that the average number of personal attendants among upper-class Romans seems to have been much higher than it was in Athens. At the same time, it is possible that rich freedmen who wanted to show off bought large numbers, while aristocratic Romans were content with fewer slaves. )

# FURTHER STUDY

1. Draw a slave auction (see p. 15). Look at several pictures so as to get the dress right: rich buyers who are Roman citizens will be wearing togas. Others will only have tunics on. Someone might be inspecting the slave being sold.
2. Find out more about Julius Caesar (p. 15). You could read about him in Suetonius' *Lives of the Twelve Caesars* or Plutarch's *Fall of the Roman Republic* (both Penguin Classics), or in several modern books. Then write a play based on his capture by the pirates, trying to make his character as realistic as you can.
3. Produce a form newspaper dating to 71 BC, in the time of Spartacus' revolt (see p. 22). You can find out more about the revolt in Plutarch's 'Life of Crassus', which is in *The Fall of the Roman Republic* (Penguin Classics), or in Book I of the *Civil Wars*, by Appian (Loeb Classical Library).
4. Read the *Satyricon*, by Petronius, and turn part of it into a play. The form could act it, tape-record it, and write a newspaper review of it.
5. Find out more about freedmen (Chapter Three). Look in the *Oxford Classical Dictionary*, or an encyclopedia. Many of the characters in the *Satyricon* are freedmen. What were the advantages and disadvantages of being a freedman?
6. Find out more about Hannibal (p. 23). You might read L. Cottrell's *Enemy of Rome* (Pan) or M. Dolan's *Hannibal of Carthage* (Macdonald), or Livy's *The War with Hannibal* (Penguin Classics). Then imagine you are in Hannibal's army of invasion, and write a diary of your march over the Alps; or else imagine you are telling your grandchildren about the battle of Cannae. (You could either write or tape-record your account.)
7. Make a list of ten jobs which in the ancient world were often done by slaves (Chapters Four and Five). Find out what you can about them now. How well are they paid? Are they thought to be good jobs? (Ask your parents and teachers and their friends.)
8. Read the seventh Satire of Book I of Juvenal's *Satires* (Penguin Classics), about the arts and education in Rome. Could they be described similarly today? What differences are there?
9. Find out more about gladiators (Chapter Five). You could read J. Murrell's *Athletics, Sports and Games* (in this series) or M. Grant's *Gladiators* (Pelican). Make a wall chart illustrating and describing the different kinds of gladiators.
10. Look carefully at all the pictures of amphitheatres you can find, and then build a model one, with contests in progress.

11. Read the *Frogs* of Aristophanes, the *Bad-Tempered Man* of Menander and the *Prisoners* of Plautus (all in Penguin Classics). Then write down anything that strikes you as interesting or surprising about the behaviour or treatment of the slaves in these plays. Do they seem to you to be true to life? Do you think the three plays show any difference of attitude?

12. Read Horace, *Satires* II. 7, and *Epistles* I. 14; Cicero's letters to Tiro (translation by L. P. Wilkinson, Hutchinson University Library, pp. 104, 108 and 176); and Pliny's *Letters* I. 4 and 21, V. 19 and VIII. 16 (Penguin Classics). Then write short character sketches of Horace, Cicero and Pliny on the basis of what you have read. Do they strike you as typical Romans, especially in their treatment of slaves?

13. Find out about Victorian mill-workers (see Charles Dickens's *Hard Times*; Charles Booth's *London* (Pelican); *The Unknown Mayhew*, edited by Thompson and Yeo (Pelican)). Would you prefer to have been a Victorian mill-worker, a Roman slave, or a Greek slave? Write a short essay explaining the reasons for your choice.

14. See if you can find out what proportion of the population were slaves in the southern states of the United States of America in the last century, and on the Caribbean sugar plantations. Compare the answers with the numbers given in Chapter Eight.

15. Find out about the treatment of slaves in the southern states of the United States and/or the Caribbean sugar plantations. What differences can you find between slavery there and in the ancient world? (Look at *To Be a Slave* by Julius Lester (Puffin).)

16. A number of Latin terms have been used in the book, such as Senate, Roman Knight, Consul, Censor, Aedile, Praetor. Find out what they mean, and how the Roman constitution worked. (Look in *SPQR* by White and Kennedy (Macmillan), or Chapter 19 of *Everyday Life in Rome* by Treble and King (OUP).)

17. Find out about Spartan *helots* (see R. Barrow's *Sparta* in this series). How were they different from slaves in other parts of Greece?

18. Can you think of any group of people in the world today whom ancient Greeks or Romans would call slaves, even if we don't? If so, write down your reasons for selecting them.

19. Imagine you are a Greek or Roman slave. Write a song protesting about your life and sing it to the form.

20. Organise a debate in your form. Discuss whether slavery is wrong, and if so why. Is there anything to be said in its favour?